METROPOLITAN PETRO MOHYLA and the ORTHODOX CONFESSION OF FAITH

Andre Partykevich

Copyright © 2014 **Andre Partykevich**

All rights reserved.

ISBN: 0692272070

ISBN 13: 9780692272077

Library of Congress Control Number: 2014914410

Little Litany Press, Philadelphia, PA

Acknowledgements

This short work was originally prepared as part of a graduate seminar at the University of Illinois at Chicago. I am grateful for the advice of Professor James Cracraft who later served as the chairperson of my PhD dissertation defense committee. This work has been read, in sections, at various conferences honoring and exploring the life and work of Metropolitan Petro Mohyla. I am exceptionally grateful to the library archives of the Ukrainian Autocephalous Orthodox Church Outside Ukraine, headquartered in Houston Texas, for preserving and providing me with a copy of the original essay, which had been lost. Finally, I am grateful to my parents, Vyacheslav and Irene, who have loved and supported me in many ways.

Preface

In 1996, I was in Kyiv, Ukraine as a guest of His Holiness Filaret, Patriarch of Kyiv, and of all Rus'-Ukraine. It was the 75th anniversary of the Ukrainian Autocephalous Orthodox Church (1921), and I had been invited to lecture on a pivotal individual in that historical period, Oleksander Lototsky, minister of religion in the government of Ukraine and representative of the government to the Ecumenical Patriarchate in the revolutionary period (1918-1921). At an informal dinner hosted by Patriarch Filaret, I found myself at a table surrounded by several distinguished bishops of the Church. His Holiness, seated at the far end of the table, addressed a question to me. "Father Andre, we are considering the canonization to sainthood of Metropolitan Petro Mohyla. You are a learned priest, what do you think about this action?" Suddenly I felt the same pain, unease and discomfort that inflicted me when I had to defend my PhD dissertation in the presence of learned historians. "Well, your Holiness, such an act might be fairly controversial, as many of Mohyla's theological views were more Catholic than Orthodox." The Patriarch took a moment, and said "yes, we will have to fix that."

Thus the Orthodox Church, and in particular the Ukrainian Orthodox Church has a particular challenge when it comes to the theology and works of Metropolitan Petro Mohyla. Saints are saints in the Orthodox Church not because they led perfect, infallible lives, but because they, to the best of the abilities, imitated God, and in the words of St. Maximos the Confessor, reached *theosis* or deification. And so "by fixing," the Patriarch probably meant that the proposed canonization would emphasize the varied ecclesiastical, scholarly, and charitable good works of Mohyla, rather than emphasize his controversial, although officially accepted, theological views and writings.

Later that same year, in 1996, the Ukrainian Orthodox Church, Kyivan Patriarchate as well as the Ukrainian Orthodox Church, Moscow Patriarchate, separately proclaimed the sainthood of Metropolitan Petro Mohyla, 350 years after his death. The new saint's feast day is January 1, the day of his repose. He is also venerated as a saint by the Romanian Orthodox Church as well as the Polish Orthodox Church. There are no earthly remains of the Metropolitan. His tomb, located in the Dormition Church of the Kyiv Pecherska Lavra, was destroyed during bombing by the German forces in World War II. When I had the opportunity to visit Kyiv several years after his canonization, I went to the Dormition Church in the monastery, and quietly chanted the *megalynarion/velychann*ia (magnification hymn) to Saint Petro Mohyla. The Church had spoken, and there was no longer anything that needed to be "fixed."

After sadness joy steps forth,
After darkness light appears,
After the dry summer, there is autumn, and
in its footsteps,
Walks winter and brings times of grief.
After the winter harshness God bestows spring . . . .
[Oh] pious founder, patron of the virtuous sciences,
Delight of all learned [men], . . .
Announces even more clearly your praiseworthy position.[1]

This panegyric, *Eucharisterion, Albo Vdjacnost'*, was presented on April 1, 1632 by the students of a rhetoric class in the newly-established gymnasium at the Monastery of the Caves in Kyiv[2] to honor Archimandrite Petro

---

[1] Natalia Pylypiuk, "Eucharisterion. Albo, Vdjacnost. The First Panegyric of the Kiev Mohyla School: Its Content and Historical Context," *Harvard Ukrainian Studies*, Vol. VIII, No. 1/2 (June 1984): 61-62.

[2] I have chosen to use the spelling Kyiv instead of the better known Kiev, for the capital of Ukraine. The exception to this is when quoting directly from a source.

Archimandrite Petro Mohyla.[3] He was the founder and patron of several schools. The passage not only refers to Petro Mohyla as an important churchman for seventeenth-century Orthodoxy, but seems to also allude to Mohyla's important position in Ukrainian history, particularly Ukrainian Orthodox Church history. Following the decline in the effectiveness and morality of Orthodox clergy of the fifteenth and sixteenth centuries, the tragic Union of Brest in 1596[4], and the re-establishment of an

---

3 There are several main orthographic variations of this surname: the Romanian Movila and the Slavic versions of Mogila, Moghila, Mohila, Mohyla, etc. Stressing the country of his origin, Romanian historians prefer Movila. Russian scholars adhere to Mogila or Moghila, while Ukrainian scholars prefer Mohila or Mohyla. In all three languages, the name means hillcock, or mound, or grave. Throughout this work I have chosen to use the Ukrainian version of Mohyla, except where quoted, as used by the Ukrainian Research Institute at Harvard University. This same Institute translates Metropolitan Mohyla's first name and uses the English, Peter. It is Orthodox monastic tradition that bishops, being monastics, do not use their last names but only their first, this being their monastic tonsured name, along with their Monastery, or if a bishop, their diocese. Thus, the bishop's full name, in ecclesiastical terminology, would be, Metropolitan Petro (Mohyla) of Kyiv. I have chosen to use the modern Ukrainian version of the Metropolitan's first name, Petro, throughout this work, except where quoted. This, I believe, keeps him in his Ukrainian, Slavic milieu where he spent the majority of his ecclesiastical career.

4 The Union of Brest (1596) was an act of unification by most of the bishops of the Orthodox Church in Rus'-Ukraine, to enter into full Eucharistic communion with the Pope of Rome and place the Church under the authority of the Pope, while maintaining Eastern rituals and Orthodox theology. For a very balanced treatment of this topic, by an Eastern Catholic, see *Crisis and Reform: The Kyivan Metropolitanate, the Patriarchate of Constantinople, and the Genesis of the Union of Brest*, by Boris Gudziak (1999).

Orthodox hierarchy in Ukraine in 1620, Petro Mohyla brings "light and joy" to the nation and her Church.

Engraving of Mohyla in the book *Eucharistion* (1632) published by the Kyivan Pecherska Lavra Monastery Press.

Metropolitan Petro Mohyla of Kyiv remains to this day a controversial figure in Ukrainian and Russian national and church history as well as in the history of the Orthodox Church. During the seventeenth century, the ecumenical Orthodox Church saw a decline in Orthodox scholarly thought, as well as traditional Orthodox consciousness. Petro Mohyla's views and writings were relatively consistent with Eastern Orthodox thought of that time. This period was one of both rapid rise in scholarly theological thought in the West and the failure in Orthodox response to a burgeoning doctrinal development in the Roman Catholic and Protestant Churches. Mohyla presented in his writings, particularly in his *Orthodox Confession of Faith*, popular and broadly accepted Orthodox positions at the time. Using what Mohyla believed to be the best available resources and tools, he presented the Christian world intelligent answers to questions concerning the Orthodox faith.

This essay examines the life of Metropolitan Petro Mohyla, whom historians often offer contradictory data about. Petro Mohyla's theology of the Eastern Orthodox Church is analyzed. However, it is also important to review not only Orthodox theological thought of the seventeenth century, but also the scholarly doctrinal thought of Roman Catholicism during this era. This is the theology closest to the mind, if not the spirit, of Petro Mohyla. Finally, an analysis of Mohyla's *Orthodox Confession of Faith* will be compared to patristic Orthodoxy.

Metropolitan Makary, the celebrated Russian Church historian of the nineteenth century, commented that "[T]he name of Petro Mohyla is one of the greatest ornaments in the history of the Church." This is from the view that Mohyla had been, at different times, both severely criticized and highly praised for his life and works. There's also the belief that a detailed study is needed of his controversial *Confession*, which remains an accepted doctrinal statement for the Orthodox Church written by a leader of the highly influential Kyivan Church.

A portrait of Metropolitan Mohyla published in Kyiv 1882

A short biography of Petro Mohyla

Petro Mohyla, son of Moldovan Prince Simeon and Hungarian Princess Marguerita, was born on December 21, 1596.[5] Although this date is disputed by many historians, the most respected Mohyla biographer, Stefan Golubev, cites the date as 1596 from the various panegyrics given to Petro Mohyla on his name's day. The panegyrics state that Mohyla was born not long before the feast of the Nativity of Christ on December 21, the date upon which the memory of the fourteenth century Metropolitan Peter is celebrated and, in his honor, Mohyla was given the same name as the Metropolitan.[6]

Professor Arcady Joukovsky provides two interesting and varied legends concerning the origin and genealogy of the Mohyla family. The first is a Polish-created legend that lists the family as originating in Rome. The second is a Romanian legend that presents a story of the Mohyla family as members

---

[5] The Julian calendar was in use by civil and ecclesiastical authorities throughout Ukraine at this time. All dates in this work, unless noted, are given according to that calendar.

[6] Stefan Golubev, *Kievski Mitropolit i Ego Spodvizhniki* (Kyiv, Korchak-Novitski, 1883), pp. 6-8. S. Rozhdestvens'ky gives Mohyla's birth date as 1590. Popivchak notes that a Romanian historian, Nicholas Iorga gives the year 1597 as Mohyla's birth date. Disagreeing with Popivchak, Joukovsky states that Iorga gives the same date as Golubev. The date is the feast day of Peter, the sainted Metropolitan of Kyiv and all Rus. The fourteenth century Metropolitan is perhaps best known for the transfer of his Metropolitan see from Vladimir to Moscow in 1325.

of a warrior class.⁷ There is no direct evidence of the exact birthplace of Petro Mohyla. However, it is often assumed by most historians that the future Kyivan Metropolitan was born in the ancient Moldovan capital of Iasi (Jassy). A foundation for this presumption is built upon the fact that Iasi was the home of the prince and princess, Mohyla's parents. Nonetheless, this is only speculation.

A Romanian icon of the Metropolitan

---

7 Arcady Joukovsky, *Petro Mohyla y Pytannia Iednosty Tserkov* (Paris: Ukrains'ky Viln'y Universytet, 1969), pp. 48-52.

Very little is known about the early life of Petro Mohyla prior to his monastic tonsure in 1608. It is probable that young Petro was schooled in the basics of Orthodoxy, as well as the rudimentary skills of reading and writing. Golubev writes that the early education of Petro was probably under the guidance of tutors from the L'viv Brotherhood school, which had a cordial relationship with the Mohyla family.[8]

Golubev also raises questions of whether Petro actually studied at the academy or if members of the school tutored him at his home in Iasi.[9] Joukovsky states that there is a possibility that Petro was sent at an early age to study in Western Europe, although there is no documentation for this.[10] There are also no historical facts leading to the widely held assumption that Petro Mohyla studied at the Sorbonne in Paris. A Soviet scholar, Medynskii, states that the usual university education in the seventeenth century lasted from six to eight years and Mohyla was an officer in the Polish Army at 20; so "when did he have the time to study at the University?" He was not a university student at the age of 12 or 13. This is a flattering statement made

---

8 Golubev, p. 19.
Golubev cites a letter of Petro's mother, Marguerita in which she invites the members of the L'viv brotherhood school to instruct her son, who was later to be sent to L'viv to study. Golubev, p. 16n.54.

9 Golubev, p. 16.

10 Joukovsky, p. 56.

in later biographies written to improve the image of Petro Mohyla.[11]

Postage stamp honoring Mohyla issued by
the government of Ukraine in 1996

The need to determine the nature and location of Mohyla's primary education is self-evident with regards to his later theological writings and pronouncements. Having been educated in Western Europe would provide logical roots for Mohyla's Western-flavored theology. By the way of fact, one can proceed safely only with Golubev's statement that "[w]e have, regretfully, almost no positive knowledge about

---

11 E. Medyns'kii, *Brats'ki Shkoly Ukrainy i Bilorussi v xvi–xvii st.*, p. 113. as quoted in Jouvovsky, p. 57.

the primary education and school years of the life of our Metropolitan."[12]

Simeon Mohyla succeeded his brother Jeremiah (Yeremia) to the throne of Moldova in 1606. Golubev states that Simeon was poisoned and his death marks the end of the Moldovan chapter of the Mohyla family. The widow, Marguerita, sought and gained refuge for herself and her son Petro in L'viv at the Orthodox Brotherhood. The Orthodox Brotherhood had been the recipient of financial and moral support from the neighboring princes of Moldova and Wallachia for years. Popivchak remarks that a strong "possibility points to the conclusion that Peter studied at the respected Brotherhood school."[13] Therefore it is presumed that Petro spent the years 1606(7)-1610(12) at the Orthodox Brotherhood school in L'viv. This leaves at least a five-year gap before the future Metropolitan re-appears under the tutorage of Polish crown chancellor Hetman Stanislaw Zholkywski (Zolkiewskii) in 1617. The question again arises concerning the nature and whereabouts of Mohyla's activity from 1612 until 1617. The answer most often given, although not documented, is that his studies were completed in foreign universities.[14]

---

12 Golubev, p. 16.
13 Ronald P. Popivchak, *Peter Mohila, Metropolitan of Kiev (1633-47). Translation and Evaluation of His "Orthodox Confession of Faith" (1640)* (Washington D.C.: The Catholic University of America, 1975), p. 5.
14 Golubev, p. 19.

A postage stamp honoring Mohyla (Movila) issued
by the government of Moldova in 2006

A rather interesting debate regarding Mohyla's foreign university studies is presented by Father Popivchak in his *Peter Mohyla, Metropolitan of Kiev 1632-1647; Translation and Evaluation of His "Orthodox Confession of Faith"* (1640). Popivchak states that although all leading Ukrainian, Russian, French and Romanian scholars agree that Mohyla studied in the West, it is his belief that this is a myth that is "convenient, for it enables scholars to explain Mohila's later 'pro-Western' leanings in both theology and politics. . . "¹⁵ Popivchak believes that this notion is actually unwarranted.

The following respected historians do conclude that Mohyla studied in Western Europe: Golubev, Doroshenko, Kostomarov, Ternovsky, Schurat, Hrushevs'ky, Haevs'ky, Vlasovs'ky, Kartashev, Michalcescu, Erbiceanu, and Picot. Popivchak bases his contrary thoughts on the writings of Martin Jugie. Jugie states how "[s]ome historians, based on an oral tradition preserved at Kyiv, aver that Peter had completed his education abroad; but they are quite embarrassed, in the absence of any proof, to say where he went. Some have him traveling to Holland, others tell us that he studied at the University of Paris; still others mention further sites."[16] Popivchak, however, believes that Mohyla never left the realm of the Polish kingdom, probably attending the University of Cracow.

The concept that Mohyla studied abroad is also disputed by the respected Russian church historian Kharlampovich.[17] In his conclusion, Popivchak states that:

> If one remembers that Peter became the protégé of the Crown Chancellor of Poland in

---

15 Popivchak, p. 6.

16 Martin Jugie, *Pierre Moghila*, pp. 2063-4. as quoted in Popivchak, p. 8.

17 K. Kharlampovich, *Malorossiikoe Vliianie na Velykorysskyiu Tserkovnyiu Zhyzn* (Kazan: 1914), p. 48.

> 1616 or 1617, who must have had social and political ties in Cracow, it is not unreasonable to theorize that Peter attended this University. In the absence of any clear documentation on Peter's higher education, it may be well to bury the myth of his Parisian sojourn.[18]

Popivchak also, of course, lacks any documentation for this theory.

Petro Mohyla's relationship with King Sigismund's Chancellor and Hetman of the Polish Army, Stanislaw Zholkywsky, lasted only a few years, from 1616 or 1617 to 1620. This relationship shows the attachment of Mohyla to the Polish Crown.[19] The sporadic but intense wars between Poland and Moscow in the first half of the seventeenth century offered Petro the chance to demonstrate his orientation; he supported Poland and opposed Moscow. Mohyla's selection as Archimandrite of the Kyivan Monastery of the Caves (Pecherska Lavra) in 1627 and the Metropolitan of Kyiv in 1632 was made and confirmed by the King and Senate of Poland.

---

18 Popivchak, p. 8.
19 In 1569 the Polish-Lithuanian Commonwealth was established at the Union of Lublin. A large portion of Ukraine was placed under Polish rule. Kyiv was part of this territory during the time of Mohyla. Kyiv officially became part of the Tsardom of Russia after the Truce of Andrusovo in 1667.

A second postage stamp issued by the government of
Moldova featuring Mohyla's (Movila's) publishing efforts

The first definite mention of Petro Mohyla by all his biographers, according to Golubev, consists of the fact that Mohyla, prior to his priesthood, "participated in the battle of Khotyn where he fought in the ranks of the Polish Army."[20] Mohyla served in the Polish army to fight against the Turks, an enemy of his homeland, Moldova. The transition that occurred in the life of Mohyla from soldier to monk lasted several years, from 1620 to 1627.

---

20 Golubev, pp. 53-54

Coat of arms of the Mohyla family

Golubev sees the entrance of Petro into the Monastery as a result of the Polish military defeat at Tsetsora and the stalemate at Khotyn. He further proposes that Mohyla met Kyivan Metropolitan Iov (Job) Borets'ky and rector Cassian Sakovych in Kyiv, at the funeral of Cossack Hetman Petro Konashevych Sahaydachny in 1622. Various explanations are given for Mohyla's decision to enter the Caves Monastery in

Kyiv, among them the influence and suggestions of Borets'ky and Sakovych.[21] Metropolitan Iov later became the spiritual father to Mohyla. Joukovsky writes that Borets'ky had a monumental influence upon the later life of the young monastic, citing how the "active participation in ecclesiastical matters fundamentally changed the life of the Moldovan prince, who left the worldly life and received the monastic habit."[22] The first period of Petro Mohyla's life ended in 1627, commencing his years of service to the Orthodox Church in Ukraine.

Petro Mohyla entered the Pecherska Lavra Monastery in August 1627, five months after the death of Archimandrite Father Zakhary (Kopystens'ky). By Christmas of the same year Mohyla was chosen, confirmed by the King of Poland, and elevated as the new Archimandrite of the Monastery. This post was one of the most influential and powerful in the entire Slavic Orthodox world. Father Georges Florovsky[23] saw Mohyla's entrance into the Monastery and his acceptance of monastic vows, as well as his elevation to Superior, as a well-planned series of activities. As Florovskii states, "Mogila seems to have had from birth an appetite and talent

---

21 It would not have been uncommon at the time for a prince without a throne, to take monastic vows and enter a monastery.

22 Joukovsky, p. 60.

23 Father Georges Florovsky used this spelling for his works which were translated into English. I have used this spelling throughout this work except when quoting his works from the original Russian and therefore used the standard transliteration of his last name: Florovskii.

for power . . . . He probably aspired to this [the Office of Archimandrite] when he took monastic vows."[24]

Professor Joukovsky questions "the reasons and events that prompted Mohyla to be ordained and head the Pecherska Lavra?"[25] Joukovsky rejects the notion that Mohyla accepted monasticism solely for idealistic motives and the desire to serve the Church. He also rejects any notion that Mohyla was attracted to the financial benefits that were associated with the Monastery's administration. Golubev notes that the sad state of the Church in the "southern Rus" lands did not go unnoticed by Mohyla and, therefore, probably produced a sympathetic response from him. The positive works of Metropolitan Borets'ky in aiding the damaged Church probably also had a positive effect and Mohyla desired to continue his good works. Joukovsky agrees with Golubev that Mohyla's character did not fit the stereotypical cloistered monk. Joukovsky notes that it is important to remember that higher ecclesiastical positions were often held by people from aristocratic families and members of royalty.

Archimandrite Zakhary of the Monastery died on March 21, 1627. The position of Archimandrite was contended by four people. Father Feofan Boyars'ky was originally chosen as superior by the monastic community. Golubev cites three reasons that the

---

24 Georgii, Florovskii, *Puti Russkago Bogosloviia* (Paris: YMCA Press, 1983), p. 44.
25 Joukovsky, p. 60.

monks themselves did not desire Mohyla as superior. First, Mohyla was only 30 years old; too young for such a position of authority. Secondly, Mohyla was a foreigner, not a Kyivan. Choosing a foreigner was against the tradition of the Lavra. Finally, Mohyla's relationship with Archbishop Meletius (Smotryts'ky),[26] who was believed by the monastics of the Lavra to have Roman Catholic sympathies[27], had made Mohyla an undesirable candidate[28]

Despite these reasons, on September 6, 1627, the Lavra synod, composed of all the clergy and monastics of the Monastery, met in Zhytomyr and "elected as Archimandrite of the Pecherska Lavra Monastery the noble Petro Mohyla, *voivode*[29] of the Moldovan lands, a person well known."[30] This election was confirmed by King Sigismund III in a decree issued on November 29, 1627. Petro Mohyla was ordained and installed as Archimandrite on December 21 or 25, 1627. As his guide (*starets'*), Petro would have Metropolitan Iov (Borets'ky) of Kyiv, who strove to raise the educational level of their fellow churchmen through prayer, the study of theology, and the actions of good works. In a time after the Union of Brest, Borets'ky strove to

---

26 Father Florovsky notes that Mohyla and Smotryts'ky had a very close relationship because of Smotryts'ky's learnedness. Florovskii, pp. 46-47.

27 Smotryts'ky, Archbishop of Polotsk, later sided with those bishops who signed the Union of Brest, becoming a Uniate bishop.

28 Goulbev, pp. 70-73.

29 Originally a warlord and later used for a governor or prince of a territory.

30 Goulbev, p. 556.

unify all Ruthenians and Ukrainians into the unified Orthodox Church.

Memorial plaque dedicated to Mohyla located at the
National University of the Kyivan Mohyla
Academy, Kyiv, Ukraine

As Archimandrite, Petro Mohyla attempted to relieve the uncomfortable position of Orthodox Christians in Ukraine under Polish rule. With a desire to bring growth to the Lavra, Archimandrite Petro concerned himself with the financial, as well as the moral, well-being of the Monastery. Financially,

Mohyla made an attempt at regaining all of the Monastery's former assets. Desiring to create within the Monastery a spiritual and educational atmosphere, he encouraged the monastics not only to lead a holy life, but also a life of study. Acting as a leader of Orthodoxy, Mohyla worked to raise the spiritual, educational, and moral levels of his spiritual children, which had fallen following the Union of Brest in 1596.

A 19th century icon of Mohyla

It is beyond the scope of this work to discuss all of the major activities and accomplishments of Petro Mohyla while Archimandrite of the Kyivan Pecherska Lavra Monastery. Those listed by his chief biographer Golubev include the beautification of the Lavra Monastery, the glorification of the Lavra, the struggle with the non-Orthodox faiths, the printing of books, the maintenance of the Lavra as a major liturgical center, the increase of the influence of the Lavra over smaller monasteries in the area, and the transfer of the Mohyla school at the Lavra into a major educational institution.[31] In a declaration made by Mohyla at the consecration of the Dormition Church in L'viv on June 15, 1631, the future Metropolitan's deep concern for the Church is clear, as well as his formula for rectifying the grave situation of the Church:

> I, Petro Mohyla, by the grace of God, Archimandrite of the Kyivan Pecherska Lavra Monastery, see in the Orthodox Church a major problem in the souls of people due to a lack

---

[31] For a detailed view of the educational activities of Mohyla, especially in the establishment of what would be known as the Kyivan Academy, with a detailed look at the curriculum, see: Alexander Sydorenko, *The Kievan Academy in the Seventeenth Century*. For a contrasting view of the Academy, see Florovskii, pp. 50-56, which presents the Academy as very Latin, scholastically, and as breaking with all traditions of earlier schools in "West Russia." It is also important to see the special issue of "Harvard Ukrainian Studies," devoted to the Kyiv Mohyla Academy, Vol. VIII, No. 1/2, June 1984.

> of religious education . . . with the grace and help of God and my own free will, I wish to prevent the continuation of such a great loss and desire to convert those who have been lost from Orthodoxy. I have decided to establish schools so that the youth may, in all piety and science, be well schooled . . . this is to be done not for my own glory, but for the glory and honor of the Life-creating Spirit and for the benefit and joy of the Orthodox . . . .[32]

The ecclesiastical and cultural activities of Archimandrite Petro Mohyla enabled him to assume a position of major influence, not only in Slavic Orthodoxy, but also over the Orthodox Church in Poland.[33] His future would include even more power, as he was to become the Metropolitan of Kyiv.

When King Sigismund Vasa died in 1632, Orthodox Christians took the opportunity to gain rights that were lost at the Union of Brest in 1596. As Golubev notes, the request made by the Zaporizhian Cossack delegates at the election of a new Polish King at the parliamentary session on June 3, 1632: "Our nation should not suffer any more oppression,

---

[32] M. Hrushevs'ky, *Istoria Ukrainy-Rusy*. (Kyiv: 1909), Vol. II, pp. 419-20.

[33] See Peter, Potichnyj, (ed.) *Poland and Ukraine, Past and Present* (Edmonton: The Canadian Institute of Ukrainian Studies, 1980), p. 74.

and should be free to enjoy the rights guaranteed to her, the Orthodox."[34]

The same appeals were made by delegates of the Brotherhood schools. Petro Mohyla made an important place for himself among the other delegates, also appealing for the rights of the Orthodox under Polish rule. At the election of the new Polish King, Wladyslaw IV Vassa, on November 13, 1632, the new King vowed to return the rights of the Orthodox living within his realm, which had been denied since the Union of Brest.

Among the requested rights was that of the Orthodox to have their own hierarchy, a Metropolitan and four bishops with sees in L'viv, Luts'k, Peremyshl, and Mstyslav.[35] Such appointments would be ratified by the Polish King.

Before the election, however, a group of delegates on November 3, 1632 had proposed that the new Metropolitan of Kyiv be none other than Archimandrite Petro Mohyla. Forty-nine Orthodox members of the *schlachta*, the privileged noble class, signed the act, listing their second choice as Mykhailo Lozka.

Joukovsky, in reviewing several biographies of Mohyla, cites many reasons as to why Mohyla became the preferred candidate for the position of Metropolitan of Kyiv, including that Mohyla alone politically maneuvered his election. Whatever the case

---

34 Golubev, Vol. II, p. 407

35 For a detailed biography of the bishops chosen for the sees, see: Ivan Vlasovs'ky, *Narys Istorii Ukrains'koi Pravoslavnoi Tserkvy* (New York: Ukrainian Orthodox Church, 1956), Vol. II, pp. 115-128.

might be, on November 11, 1632, the new Polish King ratified Mohyla's election as Metropolitan of Kyiv. Following the King's coronation on March 14, 1633, the King described the history of the Mohyla family's faithfulness to the Polish crown and granted the rights of the Episcopal see of Kyiv to Mohyla. The King saw Mohyla as "the most virtuous person" for the office.

Professor Sevcenko of Harvard University writes that Petro Mohyla, in the tradition of the Mohyla family, was a loyal subject of the Polish crown. Sevcenko writes how:

> In Mohyla's own mind, the legitimacy of his being seated on the Kiev Metropolitan's throne rested on three fundations (sic.): (1) the inspiration by the Holy Ghost who moved the heart of His Majesty King Wladyslaw IV; (2) the blessing of the holy apostolic capital of Constantinople; and (3) the will of the whole of the Ruthenian nation.[36]

Mohyla received the blessing of the Ecumenical Patriarch of Constantinople, Cyril Lukaris. Patriarch Cyril also honored Mohyla with the title "Exarch of the holy and apostolic

---

36 Ihor Sevcenko, "The Many Worlds of Petro Mohyla," *Harvard Ukrainian Studies*, Vol. VIII, No. 1/2 (June 1984):31.

throne of Constantinople."[37] To avoid problems with the current Metropolitan of Kyiv, Isaiah Kopyns'ky[38], L'viv, rather than Kyiv, was chosen as the site for the episcopal ordination. "Archbishop Isaiah Kopyns'ky was known by monastics and the Cossacks as a loyal and firm defender of Orthodoxy, a conservative in views, and a major supporter of the views of the Tsar of Moscow," notes Ivan Vlasovs'ky.[39]

Father Florovsky has a different perspective on the conflict between Kopyns'ky and Mohyla, which ultimately resulted in Kopyns'ky's loss of office. According to Florovsky, the clash between Mohyla and Kopyns'ky was not simply a competition for position of power. It was a collision of deep-rooted convictions about the fundamental problems of ecclesiastical orientation, in both its political and cultural dimensions. "Kopyns'ky was a man . . . immersed in the traditions of Eastern theology and ascetics . . . Kopyns'ky looked to the Orthodox state of Muscovy, while Petr Mogila sought help from the Catholic

---

37 Golubev, p. 547.

38 Isaiah Kopynsky succeeded Metropolitan Iov Boretsky as Metropolitan of Kyiv in 1631. He was viewed as hostile to the Uniates, favoring Ukrainian unification with the Metropolitan of Moscow. When the Orthodox hierarchy was legalized (recognized) by the Polish King in 1632, Isaiah was forced to renounce his seat as Metropolitan. Petro Mohyla, endorsed by the Polish authorities, was then enthroned. It is interesting to note that Mohyla, and not Kopynsky, had the support of the Ecumenical Patriarchate.

39 Vlasovs'ky, Vol. II, p. 101.

kingdom of Poland."[40] Although L'viv was closer to the Polish seat of government, the ancient St. Sophia Cathedral in Kyiv was still in the hands of the Uniates[41]. The use of St. Sophia's Cathedral for the installation ceremony proved difficult. Being in L'viv, Mohyla was able to take advantage of the great sympathizers that he had in this vital city.

On Saturday, April 27, 1633, Mohyla, at the age of 36, one year older than the required age for bishops, was ordained a bishop by the exarch of the Constantinopolian Patriarch, Jeremiah Tusarovs'ky, and the Bishop of L'viv, with three other bishops. The next day Mohyla was officially elevated to the rank of Archbishop and the title "Metropolitan of Kyiv" was bestowed upon him by the Patriarchal exarch. Mohyla announced plans to re-consecrate St. Sophia's Cathedral in Kyiv, "the jewel of all Orthodoxy, the mother of all Churches in the nation."[42] Following a lengthy battle with the former Metropolitan Isaiah, the duly elected and recognized Metropolitan took his place as the Kyivan hierarch. It should be noted that according to Orthodox canon law, a bishop may be removed from his see only upon the ruling of an ecclesiastical court, composed of other bishops, usually twelve in number.[43] The former

---

40 Florovskii, p. 48.

41 Eastern rite Catholics. Considered by many to be a pejorative term, it refers to those Orthodox who united with the Pope of Rome and the Catholic Church in 1596.

42 See Joukovsky, pp. 95-99.

43 *Pedalion* (Athens: Nicolaides Kesisoglou, 1908), p. 253, Canon IX of the Council of Chalcedon, 451.

Metropolitan, now dethroned, remained in Kyiv under strict watch until his death.

Some of the major accomplishments of Mohyla as Metropolitan of Kyiv were (1) the organization of church life, (2) the return of property once held by the Orthodox currently in Uniate hands, (3) the building of new churches, and (4) the restoration of damaged churches, among them the famous St. Sophia's Cathedral and the Tithe Church in Kyiv.

Portrait of Mohyla in the Transfiguration Church in Berestove (Kyiv) Ukraine. Fresco.

Full fresco scene. Metropolitan Mohyla
can be seen in the lower left.
Transfiguration Church in Berestove (Kyiv) Ukraine.

A Sobor (council) was called by Metropolitan Mohyla in Kyiv on June 24, 1640. The Sobor was to concern itself with the lack of uniformity in liturgics in the Ukrainian Church. Held in St. Sophia's Cathedral from the 8th to the 18th of September, 1640, the Sobor was attended by the Metropolitan, representatives of the four episcopal sees, superiors of the monasteries, clergy, and laymen. The celebrated *Catechism of Mohyla*, later known as the *Orthodox Confession of Faith*, was discussed at the Sobor from the 9th to the 15th of September, 1640. The discussion was led by Father Abbot Isaiah Trofymovych Kozlovs'ky, a major contributor to the

Confession. It was decided by the Sobor to send the Catechism for official examination and approval to the Patriarch of Constantinople. A second major accomplishment of the Sobor was the later publication of the *Trebnik*,[44] or book of mysteries (sacraments) and blessings also referred to as "book of needs", which would help to combat the varied rites and the lack of liturgical uniformity within the Church.

The years as Metropolitan were marked with the same energetic activities as the years Mohyla had been Archimandrite. His activities following the re-establishment of the Ukrainian

---

44 Given throughout this publication as Trebnik, according to the transliteration of Old Church Slavonic, as opposed to the modern Ukrainian, Trebnyk. Although there has not been a comprehensive study of the *Trebnik*, for a historical and contemporary sober Orthodox view of Petro Mohyla's *Trebnik* see Timothy Ware, *Eustratios Argenti. A Study of the Greek Church Under Turkish Rule* (Oxford: Clarendon Press, 1964), pp. 69-70, 101. For a somewhat different view of Mohyla's *Trebnik* by an Eastern Catholic, see: George, A. Maloney, *A History of Orthodox Theology Since 1453* (Belmont, Mass.: Norland, 1976), pp. 36-7, Maloney has a false understanding of the Orthodox theological concepts of divine grace and *economia*. This is especially evident in his analysis: "Mogila accepts the Baptism of Roman Catholics and Protestants as valid." Bishop Kallistos (Timothy Ware) states that the Orthodox Church does not accept the baptism of non-orthodox, yet divine grace is fulfilled in the sacraments of chrismation, confession and communion given to those who had received the non-Orthodox baptism. Father Florovsky has quite a condemnatory view of the *Trebnik*: "What resulted from the *Trebnik* then was a radical and thorough 'Latinazation' of the Eastern rite . . . toward the 'Latinization' of the Liturgy Mogila stands well to the front because he promoted it on a larger scale and more systematically than anyone else. pp. 51-2.

hierarchy in 1620 are well documented.[45] The fourteen years that Mohyla was the Metropolitan of Kyiv saw the elevation of the authority of the Orthodox Church in Polish-ruled Ukraine, not only in the eyes of the Orthodox world, but also in the Polish state. The publication of various works, the most significant being the *Catechism*, helped to make Kyiv a center of Orthodox learning and the Ukrainian Church with the ability to speak with authority in the Orthodox world.

Coin issued by the government of Ukraine in 1996 featuring Mohyla. 10 Hryven

---

45 See Vlasovs'ky and Doroshenko, as well as Polons'ka-Vasylenko.

Little is known about the circumstances of Mohyla's death on January 1, 1647, except that he passed away while in office. The celebrated historian of the Ukrainian Orthodox Church, Ivan Vlasovs'ky, notes the importance of this date in the calendar of the Orthodox Church.

> On this date, January 1 [January 14, according to the Gregorian calendar], the Holy Orthodox Church calls to remembrance a Father of the Eastern Church of the fourth century, St. Basil the Great. Our historians and preachers have noticed the similarities between the Archbishop of Caesarea in Cappadocia, St. Basil, and Kyivan Metropolitan Petro Mohyla; both accepted the monastic life as young men; both fought faithfully for Holy Orthodoxy (St. Basil the Great with the Arian heretics) by formulating Orthodox dogmatic thought; both gave great service and merit in the development and regulation of divine services of the Christian faith (the liturgy of St. Basil and the doctor of liturgical rites and prayers, the Liturgicon or Service Book, Euchologian or

Trebnik of Mohyla) . . . both died having lived fifty years.[46]

In the last testament of Petro Mohyla,[47] two elements are evident. The first is spiritual: Mohyla confirms, as do many former and modern bishops, his faith in Jesus Christ and His saving grace in the next life. Granting most of his worldly possessions to the Kyivan Church, "his home granted him by the Lord God," is the second portion of Mohyla's testament.

The body of Metropolitan Petro Mohyla was brought to the Cathedral of St. Sophia, where it lay until March 19, 1647, when he was buried in the Dormition Church (part of the Pecherska Lavra) under the left *klyros*.[48] The funeral sermon was given by a former student of the Metropolitan, Yosyf Kalymon. The rector of the Kyivan College, Lazar Baranovych, would later note that a "pastor is known by his good fruits. One cannot cry enough over the loss of Mohyla; he was our father and our beloved shepherd. The beloved was received [into heaven, presumably] and we are in need of a second Mohyla."[49]

---

46 Vlasovs'ky, Vol. II, p. 107.

47 *Dukhovnoe Zaveshanie*, quoted by Joukovsky, pp. 116-117.

48 Originally referring to anyone in Church service, in modern times it refers a specific location in a church building: to the right or left of the entry into the altar area.

49 L. Baranovych, *Lutnia Appolinowa*, p. 499, as quoted in Joukovsky, p. 119.

The Orthodox Confession of the Catholic (Universal) and Apostolic Eastern Church

We turn our attention now to what Bishop Kallistos (Ware) calls "still the most Latin document ever to be adopted by an official Council of the Orthodox Church."[50] This reference is to *The Orthodox Confession of the Catholic (Universal) and Apostolic Eastern Church*, authored by Petro Mohyla. This document, which is now known by a shorter title, *Orthodox Confession of Faith*, was first known as *The Teachings of Faith of Little Rus'*. The *Confession*, which dates from 1640, has been the subject of major debate in the scholarly, historical, and ecclesiastical circles for many reasons. Deserving attention is the contention that the author of the *Confession* was not Metropolitan Mohyla, but Isaiah Kozlovs'ky, rector of Mohyla's Kyivan School. The sole source of this argument is the fact that Kozlovs'ky was acclaimed as a doctor of theology by the participants of the same Sobor of Kyiv in 1640. The reasoning is that he was so honored for actually writing the *Confession*. "This thought was initiated by Russian Metropolitan Evgenii Bolchovitinov. In agreement with him are Philaret Gumilevs'kii, Moscow Metropolitan Makariy, and V. Gruzdev,"[51] all recognized as learned Churchmen.

---

50 Timothy Ware, *The Orthodox Church*, (Middlesex: Penguin Books, 1963), p.107.

51 Popivchak, p. 16.

Mohyla's Trebnik published in 1646

Another issue under debate is the original language of the *Confession*. In general, three languages have been seriously proposed: Latin, Polish, and Ruthenian[52]. Popivchak contends

---

[52] A language spoken in the Eastern Slavic territories of the Polish-Lithuanian Commonwealth. A predecessor to modern Ukrainian and Belarusian and Rusyn.

that the original *Confession* was in a Slavonic language, Polish or Ukrainian. This question is presented by Profession Sysyn, who dismisses Popivchak's argument as "does not inspire confidence."[53] However, he does not provide any answer about the original language of the *Confession*. This question is "guessed at by Professor Sevcenko, who believes the answer is Polish or Ruthenian, rather than Slavonic or Latin."[54] Although both questions of authorship and language are important, they are both beyond the scope of this work.

The *Orthodox Confession of Faith* is a theological treatise consisting of three parts (that correspond to the three Christian virtues of faith, hope, and love) and contains 261 questions and answers concerning the Orthodox Christian faith. The document was discussed and amended in Iasi (Jassy) in Moldova in 1642. Later a Greek version was approved by the four ancient Eastern Patriarchs of the Orthodox Church. The first publication of the *Confession* was in 1667 in Greek. In question and answer form, the first and longest section (126 questions) lays out dogmatic truths of the Orthodox Church, patterned after the Nicene-Constantinopolian Creed of 381. The second part (63 questions) deals with the means of salvation, the necessity

---

53 Frank E. Sysyn, "Peter Mohyla and the Kiev Academy in Recent Western Works: Divergent Views on Seventeenth Century Ukrainian Culture," *Harvard Ukrainian Studies*, Vol. VIII, No. 1/2 (June 1984), p. 156.
54 Sevcenko, p. 25.

of grace and prayer, the spiritual and temporal works of mercy, along with an explanation of the Lord's Prayer and the Sermon on the Mount (the Beatitudes). The final section (72 questions) gives a summary of Christian morality, the virtues and the major sins, and concludes with an explanation of the Ten Commandments or Decalogue.

Petro Mohyla's *Confession* was written in direct reaction to a confession composed by the Patriarch of Constantinople, Cyril Lukaris (1572-1638). Lukaris' experience as a representative at the Union of Brest in 1596 led him to combat the Roman influence in the Orthodox Church by producing a *Confession*, first published in Geneva in 1629, that is distinctively Calvinist. The Mohyla work, perhaps in direct response to Lukaris and certain Protestant forces, was based extensively on Roman Catholic texts. Although the document was approved at an Orthodox Council and has remained on the list of major Orthodox doctrinal statements since 787,[55] it was first revised by a Greek, Meletius Syrigos, exarch of the Ecumenical Patriarch of Constantinople. Mohyla, having, in Ware's opinion, been educated by the Jesuits, "drew particularly on the Catechism of Canisus[56], so that in structure and arrangement, as also in its general approach and spirit, the work corresponds closely to Roman Catholic manuals current at

---

[55] Ware, *The Orthodox Church*, p. 211.
[56] St. Peter Canisius, a Jesuit Roman Catholic priest, wrote his triple Catechism in 1557-1558

the time."⁵⁷ For Timothy Ware, the *Confession* of Mohyla "represents the high-water mark of Latin influence upon Orthodox theology."⁵⁸

Ecumenical Patriarch of Constantinople,
Hieromartyr Cyril Lucaris

---
57 Ware, *Eustratios Argenti*, p. 11.
58 Ibid., p. 13.

Mohyla's *Orthodox Confession* first appeared in 1640, when it was submitted by Mohyla to a Church Council in Kyiv for discussion and endorsement. At Kyiv, the Council criticized the draft on a number of points, especially concerning the origin of the soul, where Mohyla is extremely Augustinian in his presentation. A Council at Iasi convened by Mohyla's friend, the Moldovan Prince Basil, reviewed the document. Bishop Meletios Syrigos, one of the most remarkable Orthodox theologians of the seventeenth century, had the task of conforming the *Confession* to current Orthodox standards. Florovsky states that Mohyla:

> introduced various amendments. Most of his changes were actually stylistic . . . Mohyla had followed the Latin Vulgate, which meant that some of his citations were not in the Septuagint, or were so differently phrased that to retain them would have made the *Confession* highly inappropriate for Orthodox believers.[59]

It is confusing that Mohyla was not pleased with the amendments that Syrigos, acting as a representative of the Council, made to the *Confession*. Few people, including the Eastern patriarchs and Mohyla himself, even following their approval of the

---

59 Florovskii, p. 51.

work, desired to publish the document. A shorter version of the original work was published, the so-called *Brief Catechism*, aimed at a different audience "for the instruction of young people."

The style of the Catechism remains Roman Catholic. Syrigos, having trained in Padua, removed the major Latin adherences, yet left the presentation of the *Confession* in its original form. On this topic, Father Florovsky makes the finest analogy:

> It was not so much the doctrine, but the manner of presentation that was, so to speak, erroneous, particularly the choice of language and the tendency to employ any and all Roman weapons against Protestantism even when not consonant in full or part with Orthodox presuppositions.[60]

Florovsky labels Mohyla and his Catechism "crypto-Romanist," leaving an impression that Orthodoxy is a refined version of Catholicism in an Eastern form.

An Eastern Catholic view of Mohyla and his *Confession* has a different outlook. Father Maloney sees the *Confession* as having "a very relative authority, remaining a classic mingling of 'Byzantine Orthodoxy' and 'Westernization'."[61]

---

60 Ibid., p. 52-3.
61 Maloney, p. 33-35.

Although the four Patriarchs of the East stated in an official act that the *Confession* "conforms to the dogmas of the Church of Christ, it is in full accord with the holy canons and there is nothing in it that the Church cannot accept," Mohyla's *Confession* remains a debatable document. Patriarch Ioakim of Moscow (1685) approved the Slavonic translation, which was published in Moscow in 1696 by order of Tsar Peter the Great and with the approbation of Patriarch Adrian, Ioakim's successor, who referred to it as a "book divinely inspired."

On the Eucharist

Many of Mohyla's positions and interpretations in the *Confession* are highly controversial. One of the most debated of these concerns the Eucharist. Question 106, from the first section of the *Confession*, is entitled "On Faith." It concerns the mystery of the sacrament of Holy Communion or the Eucharist. Mohyla, providing a brief answer to the question "what is the third mystery?" states that "it is the Eucharist or body and blood of Christ the Lord, under the form of bread and wine and the real presence."[62] The answer to Question 107 elaborates on the theology of the Eucharist, as well as the liturgical theology surrounding the Divine Liturgy.

---

62 This section from page 62, as well as further citations from the *Confession* of Petro Mohyla, are from a translation into English made by Ronald Popivchak, from a Latin version of Malvy/Miller. This is the only complete translation of the work that, although Professor Sysyn labels as "clumsy," is available to this author.

Mohyla states that only a priest, one who was validly ordained, may administer this sacrament.[63] Also necessary for the celebration of the liturgy is an altar with an antimension.[64] Third, Mohyla states that "proper matter, pure leavened bread of wheat and wine" are necessary. Fourth, Mohyla makes the statement that the priest must, at the time of consecration, have the intention to celebrate the Liturgy, and believe in the transubstantiation of the bread and wine into the body and blood of Christ, through the operation of the Holy Spirit.

Mohyla, at this point, provides a lengthy explanation and scriptural defense of the real presence of Christ in the Eucharist, as well as an argument for transubstantiation occurring at the words of Institution (*Anamnesis*) in the Liturgy: "This is my body . . . This is my blood." His answer continues with three purposes for receiving the sacrament of Holy Communion. First, is an affirmation of

---

63 The Orthodox Church prefers the term "mystery" when referring to the Eucharist and the other "sacraments" and blessings administered by the Church. Because Popivchak uses the term "sacrament", for the sake of consistency, I have chosen to use the same term.

64 An Antimension (antimins) is a cloth laid upon an altar, which usually depicts the removal of Christ from the Cross and always has a relic of a saint sewn into a pocket on the reverse. It is signed by the bishop who consecrated it, usually performed on Holy or Great Thursday. It is customary for newly installed diocesan bishops to sign each antimension in his diocese as he visits the various parishes. As a general rule, a priest can't celebrate the Divine Liturgy on an antimension signed by a deceased bishop or a bishop who is no longer functioning as a diocesan bishop. This is vital as many parishes were transferred from being governed by an Orthodox bishop to being governed by a Uniate bishop.

41

faith, as stated in I Corinthians 11:26, "For as often as you shall eat this bread and drink from this chalice, you shall show the death of the Lord, until He comes." Secondly is that the Eucharist affects a propitiation for the sins of the living, as well as the dead. Finally, that the reception of the Eucharist provides the Christian with freedom from all temptation of the Devil, since the recipient now becomes the Temple of Christ.

Title page of Mohyla's Sluzhebnyk i Trebnik, 1632 edition
Held at the Vernadsky National Library in Kyiv

There are three major errors in Mohyla's answer to question 107 concerning the Eucharist, which remain even in the revised version of the *Confession*. The first regards his statement of "proper matter." Mohyla correctly states that, in accordance with Orthodox scriptural and liturgical theology, "pure leaven bread of wheat and wine, devoid of any other substance, only must be used." Mohyla makes an exception for the addition of water to the chalice, which is later added at the prothesis or preparation of bread and wine, and before the Communion of the clergy, when hot water is added, to fulfill the scriptural passage. "But one of the soldiers with a spear opened His side, and immediately there came forth blood and water (St. John 19:34)."

The Orthodox theologian of the late seventeenth century and early eighteenth century, Eustratios Argenti of Chios, criticizes the scholastic use of the word matter or form when discussing bread and wine of the Eucharist or other necessary material parts of a Sacrament, such as water for Baptism. To talk in such terms, he argues, is to introduce naturalistic and Aristotelian explanations into sacramental theology. It is to apply the language of the natural sciences to the supernatural mysteries of the Divine. He says that

> We are astonished that there can have been found men, professing theology and with a reputation for wisdom, who desire to explain the supernatural things, seeking in them 'matter and form,' terms unknown and unheard of in the Christian theology of the Catholic 'Universal' Church. [65]

Archimandrite Kyprian in his celebrated book *Evcharistia* (Eucharist), while discussing bread and wine, refrains from labeling them in the scholastic manner, except for introducing the topic as "*Veshchestvo dlia Liturgii*," (substance or matter for the Liturgy).[66] His two-page description and explanation does not use the terms "matter" or "substance;" he simply calls them bread and wine with water. What may seem petty to many Christians is viewed by the Orthodox as an important point, for by using foreign terms the theologian denies Eastern thought associated with Orthodox theology.

A second major point of contention with Mohyla's discussion of the Eucharist in the *Confession* is the necessity of the priest's "intention" to celebrate the Divine Liturgy. It is part of Orthodox theology that every priest, as well as every Orthodox Christian, must, before any act of prayer or any

---

65 Ware, *Eustratios Argenti*, p. 110.
66 Kyprian, *Evkharystiia* (Paris: YMCA Press, 1947), pp. 139-140.

reception of the Sacraments, be in a state of grace.[67] The priest should, for his own salvation and efficacy of the Eucharist upon his own soul, be in a pious state. The moral state of the priest does not affect the Sacrament, however. Although Mohyla does not state this precisely in his *Confession*, there is a hint of this concept from Latin theology: that the Eucharist is effective to the recipient, whether or not he be in a state of grace; i.e., ready to receive Holy Communion.[68] It is the Orthodox belief that, if a valid Eucharist is received by an unworthy recipient, the Eucharist, although losing none of its sanctity, has no affect upon the receiver until he or she make corrections to their life and be in a state of proper reception.

The Latin doctrine of intention is called heretical and blasphemous by Eustratios Argenti. In a commentary concerning the theology of the Orthodox Church, as explained by Argenti, Timothy Ware comments that it appears in the writings of Argenti (from the eighteenth century) that his criticism of the Latin doctrine of intention is not an innovative one, but one that was probably criticized by other Orthodox scholars. To ensure a valid Sacrament, says Argenti, two things are required: (1) a validly ordained minister of proper canonical status, and (2) the correct celebration of the Sacrament.

---

67 See Kyprian, pp. 137-138.
68 See Jaroslav, Pelikan, *The Growth of Medieval Theology 500-1300* (Chicago: The University of Chicago Press, 1978), p. 204.

> The celebrant's intention is sufficiently indicated by his recitation of the required outward actions; to insist also on some inward intention or assent is to render it for even uncertain whether a sacrament has been validly celebrated, for who, save God, can be sure precisely what is going on in the celebrant's mind.[69]

It is, of course, difficult to determine whether or not Petro Mohyla knew of such Orthodox teachings concerning the "intention" concept. What seems obvious, however, is that he chose the Latin explanation.

The third concern in Mohyla's *Confession* revolves around the term "transubstantiation." The issue concerns the use of the term "transubstantiation" when referring to the change that occurs during the Liturgy when bread and wine, mixed with water, become the body and blood of Christ. Mohyla states in the answer to question 107 of the *Confession*: "The real substance of the bread and the substance of the wine be transubstantiated into the real body and blood of Christ through the operations of the Holy Spirit."

One of the first people to speak of transubstantiation was Pope Alexander III in a work prepared around 1140.

---

69 Ware, *Eustratios Argenti*, p. 137.

Metropolitan Petro Mohyla and the Orthodox Confession of Faith

Three-quarters of a century later, the Fourth Lateran Council in 1215 promulgated the dogma that "body and blood [of Jesus Christ] was truly contained in the sacrament of the Altar under the outward appearance of bread and wine, the bread having been transubstantiated into the body and the wine into the blood."[70] Following the upheaval of the Reformation, the Council of Trent in 1551 reaffirmed transubstantiation with the statement: "This change [of bread and wine into body and blood] has conveniently and appropriately been called transubstantiation by the Holy Catholic Church."[71]

Patriarch Cyril Lukaris speaks contemptuously of the concept of transubstantiation in his *Confession*, which "creates Jesus Christ out of a piece of bread or crumb." He goes on to state that the "presence of Christ in the Eucharist is such as faith presents and offers to us, not such as the vainly invented Doctrine of Transubstantiation (metousiosis) teaches."[72]

The Patriarch of Jerusalem, Dositheos, writing in the seventeenth century, also has Latinisms concerning the Eucharist, which are apparent in his *Confession*, yet which are less serious than those of Mohyla. When discussing the Eucharist, Dositheos employs not only the term *metousiosis*, but also the scholastic distinction between accidents and substance.

---

70 Pelikan, pp. 203-204.

71 Ibid., p. 204.

72 From the *Confession* of Lukaris cited in Ware, *Eustratios Argenti*, p. 9.

Dositheos writes: "after the consecration of the bread and wine, the bread is changed, transubstantiated, converted, and transelemented into the true Body of the Lord . . . and the wine . . . into the true Blood of Christ."[73]

The Patriarch adds, however, that the term *metousiosis* must not be taken as describing the manner of the change, for he states that "this is incomprehensible and cannot possibly be described; it rather indicates the reality of the change." The *Confession* of Patriarch Dositheos was formally ratified by the Council of Jerusalem in 1672. An eminent Greek theologian of the eighteenth century, Eustratios Argenti of Chios, is much more reserved than Dositheos in his use of Latin terminology. Argenti writes: "Instead of the flesh and blood of the Passover Lamb, the bread and wine of the Eucharist were delivered to us, transelemented through prayer and spiritual blessing into the Body and Blood of Our Lord Jesus Christ."[74]

These examples of the term "transubstantiation" were written both before and after the *Confession* of Petro Mohyla. St. John of Damascus, writing in the eighth century, perhaps, provides the best Orthodox explanation. "If you inquire how this happens, it is enough for you to learn, that it is through the Holy Spirit. . . . We know nothing more than this, that

---

[73] The *Confession* of Dositheos is translated into English in J. N. Robertson, *The Acts and Decrees of the Synod of Jerusalem*. (London: Thomas Baker, 1899).

[74] Ware, *Eustratios Argenti*, p. 109.

Metropolitan Petro Mohyla and the Orthodox Confession of Faith

the word of God is true, active, and omnipotent, but in its manner of operation unsearchable."[75]

This section from *Exposition of the Orthodox Faith* by St. John is also quoted in a longer catechism composed by Metropolitan Philaret of Moscow in 1839. In patristic and current Orthodox theology, the belief remains that certain elements of the faith are better left undescribed, for when one borrows foreign terminology to describe the divine, one loses the very essence of what is believed.

Taken singularly, some of the erroneous points in Mohyla's statements concerning the Eucharist may appear of minor importance. However, it is this in their cumulative effect that they produce a serious distortion of the whole nature of the Sacrament, for they borrow Latin terminology to describe the Orthodox belief surrounding the Sacrament.

It is also important to note that in the original version of the *Confession*, Petro Mohyla stated that the change of bread and wine into the body and blood of Christ takes place during the Divine Liturgy at the words of Institution uttered by the priest. In the revised edition, adopted at the Council of Iasi, the *Confession* was changed to conform to an accepted Orthodox belief about the time that the change takes place in

---

75 (St.) John of Damascus, "Exposition of the Orthodox Faith" in *The Nicene and Post-Nicene Fathers*, edited by W. Sanday, Vol IX (Grand Rapids, Michigan: Eerdman's Publishing Co., 1979), p. 83.

the Eucharist, that moment being at the *epiclesis*.[76] The *epiclesis*, or invocation of the Holy Spirit upon the gifts, takes place following the words of Institution, when the priest uses these words:

> And make this bread the Precious Body of Thy Christ.
> And that which is in this Chalice, the Precious Blood of Thy Christ,
> Changing Them by Thy Holy Spirit.
> Amen! Amen! Amen![77]

Concerning the Departed

Questions 57-68 of part one of Petro Mohyla's *Confession*, entitled "On Faith," concern the departed, their place in the cosmos, as well as the benefit of prayers for the dead. Mohyla states that on the day of judgment, each person will receive "according to his works, eternal and perfect payment." Orthodox writers of the seventeenth century, including Mohyla, left many things concerning the particular judgment in need of further clarification. Roman Catholic and

---

[76] The idea that the bread and wine are changed at a precise moment during the Divine Liturgy is also a subject of concern for many Orthodox theologians. In the opinion of most Orthodox theologians, simply stating that the change occurs at some point during the celebration of the Liturgy, from the celebration of the *Prothesis* to the reception of Holy Communion, is enough.

[77] *Sluzhebnik*, Kyiv:1883, p. 156-157.

Orthodox theology generally agree in affirming that on the last day, Christ will come again in power and great glory to judge the dead and the living. However, in addition to this general judgment, at the end of the world there is also a particular judgment immediately after the death of each person, at which his or her eternal destiny is decided.

Roman theology teaches that there is such a particular judgment. After death, departed souls are judged forthwith and go to heaven, hell, or purgatory; the saints to enjoy their full reward, the damned to receive their full punishment, and the souls in purgatory to undergo a period of expiatory suffering and purification before they are completely admitted to the vision of God.[78]

Orthodox theology is far less clear. Timothy Ware notes that Methodius III, Patriarch of Constantinople (1668-1671), denies altogether "that there is a particular judgment." Petro Mohyla in the *Confession* definitely affirms the existence of a particular judgment in the answer to question 61, "therefore, there is a particular judgment." One point almost all Orthodox seem to agree upon in their dissenting from the Roman Catholic view is that the saints do not at once enter upon their perfect blessedness, nor are the wicked received at once into the fullness of their torment.

---

78 See, Jacques Le Goff, *The Birth of Purgatory* (Chicago: The University of Chicago Press, 1981).

Petro Mohyla writes that

> Before the final judgment, neither the just nor sinners receive the full reward for their works; nevertheless, they are not all in one and the same state, nor are they all sent to the same place. . . . The souls of the just, though they are in heaven, have not received their full crown before the final judgment, nor do the souls of the damned suffer their full punishment, it is only after the last judgment that their souls, reunited with their bodies, will receive in full, the crown of glory or the punishment due to them.[79]

Insofar as the *Confession* assigns souls to different places before the last day, it states something that most Orthodox would deny. "But practically all Orthodox" states Ware, "would agree with it when it states that neither just nor wicked receives their reward in full before the resurrection of the body."[80]

Petro Mohyla, in the original version of the *Confession*, maintained that there is a third place for departed souls, apart from heaven and hell; but he stands alone in this belief.[81]

---

[79] Popivchak, p. 47-48, 50-51.

[80] Ware, *Eustratios Argenti*, p. 143.

[81] See, Constantine Cavarnos, *The Future Life According to Orthodox Teaching*, (Etna, California: Center for Traditionalist Orthodox Studies, 1985), p. 23.

Other Orthodox writers speak only of two places, heaven and hell; most go out of their way specifically to deny the existence of purgatory. Meletius Syrigos, in a later revised version of Mohyla's *Confession*, makes the following statement:

> Question: Perhaps men die who are midway between the saved and the damned?
> Answer: There are no men in this position.
>
> Question: What should we believe about the fire of purgatory?
> Answer: This fire is not mentioned in Scripture anywhere, nor does Scripture say anywhere that there is a temporal punishment which purifies the soul after death. Indeed, it was for this reason that the opinion of origin was condemned by the Church at the second Council of Constantinople. [553][82]

It should be noted that the third century theologian Origin was condemned for teaching that the torments of hell are not eternal. Between Abraham's bosom and the torment of

---
82 Ware, *Eustratios Argenti*, p. 143-144.

Hades, writes Meletios, Patriarch of Alexandria in the early seventeenth century, we are taught that there is a kind of chaos, but no purgatory.

Concerning the benefit of prayer for the departed, Mohyla, in a revised *Confession* as adopted at Iasi, writes:

> After death, the soul cannot perform any work whereby it may procure release from the bonds of hell. Its release is affected solely by the Holy Liturgies, the prayers, and the alms of the living. ... The Church has good reason to offer the bloodless sacrifice on behalf of the departed souls and to send up prayers to God for the forgiveness of their sins. But the departed do not purify themselves by the suffering which they undergo.[83]

Petro Mohyla follows the standard Roman teaching here, which would later be changed by Meletios Syriogos. In the words of Timothy Ware, "[i]t sometimes happens that the souls of sinners are released from hell, yet this release is not secured through any penance or satisfaction which the departed

---

83 Popivchak, p. 48-50.

themselves render, but is brought about by the prayers which the living offer at their behalf."[84]

Archimandrite Chrysostomos, an Orthodox theologian of the modern day, wrote that "Few subjects in religious thought are so compelling as that of the future life, a life after death."[85] In historical and modern theology, the Orthodox Church has become the domain of speculation and creative presumption. Many Fathers of the Church, as well as Scripture to a large part, are silent about the afterlife and reticent in their approach to this topic. Unfortunately, Mohyla once again, for whatever reason, chose to explain, in Roman terms, that which the Orthodox profess is unexplainable.

On Baptism

Another point of contention for many Orthodox theologians is Mohyla's writings on the ministration of Baptism. In Christendom today, there are three different ways in which Baptism is administered: (1) Immersion; (2) Affusion or Infusion, when water is poured over candidate's forehead; and (3) Aspersion, when water is not poured, but sprinkled on the candidate's forehead.

---

84 Ware, *The Orthodox Church*, p. 258-259 and Ware, *Eustratios Argenti*, p. 150.
85 Cavarnos, p. 7.

Baptism by immersion was the normal practice in the early Church, while Baptism by affusion was allowed in case of necessity. Immersion, as practiced in the early Church, is recorded in the *Didache*, the *Shepherd of Hermas*, as well as in the writings of Tertullian, St. Basil, and St. Jerome.[86] The Orthodox Church today, except in some instances, continues to follow the ancient practice of immersion. Baptism by aspersion is usually not recognized by the Orthodox Church.

From the twelfth century onward, the Latin Church has come by degrees to abandon the rite of immersion. Timothy Ware believes this occurred because affusion was much more convenient than immersion. By the fourteenth century, Orthodox began to notice the abandonment of immersion by the Western church. Petro Mohyla, in his *Confession*, together with his *Little Catechism* of 1645, treats immersion and affusion as alternatives, standing on equal levels. According to Ware, the passage concerning Baptism by affusion in Mohyla's *Confession* was corrected by Syrigos, so that the Greek version of 1642 speaks only of Baptism by immersion. The regular usage of affusion, especially in the Slavic Church, seems to have crept into the Orthodox Church from either ignorance, convenience, or Latin influence.

---

[86] See, Henry Chadwick, *The Early Church* (London: Penguin Book, 1967)

Concerning the Trebnik of Mohyla

The *Trebnik* of Petro Mohyla also contains numerous differences with standard Orthodox thought and practice. Although these are beyond the topic of this work, they bear mentioning. The first concerns the reception of non-Orthodox into the Orthodox Church. In an analysis by Wenger, Roman Catholics desiring to enter the Orthodox Church were not required to receive the Sacrament of Chrismation.[87] They were received with the Sacraments of Confession and Communion, stating that this "regularized" their Baptism and Confirmation. Conversely, it was the practice of the Orthodox Church, in Constantinople and Jerusalem, to administer the Sacrament of Baptism and Chrismation to Roman Catholic converts.

It is perhaps the Sacrament of Confession as it appears in the Mohyla *Trebnik* that has had the longest impact upon the Orthodox Church. Petro Mohyla adopted a Latin form of absolution that is prayed over the penitent. The Greek formula states: "May God forgive you in this world and the next." Petro Mohyla, under Latin influence, used the following formula: "I, an unworthy priest, through the power given me by Him [Christ], forgive and absolve you from all your sins."[88] The above

---

[87] See, A. Wenger, "La reconciliation des heretiques dans l'Eglise Russe," *Revue des Etudes Byzantines*, Vol. XII (1954), pp. 144-175.

[88] Ware, *The Orthodox Church*, p. 297.

Latin practice remains in most of the Slavic Orthodox world and can still be found in most ritual books used by the clergy.

Another concern over Mohyla's theology is raised by Father Florovsky: "Mogila did not see any insurmountable differences of doctrine. *Filioque and per filium* varied only in the phrasing. . . . The only serious difficulty was papal supremacy."[89] Of all the sources this writer consulted, Father Florovsky is the only one to mention such contradictions of the theology concerning the procession of the Holy Spirit as understood by Mohyla. In the Popivchak version of the *Confession* we read: "The Holy Spirit proceeds from the Father alone, as principle and origin of divinity which the Savior himself teaches us, when he says: 'But when the Paraclete comes, whom I will send you from the Father, the spirit of truth, who proceeds from the Father."[90] This appears, at face value, to conform to the Orthodox understanding of the procession of the Holy Spirit.

Concluding Thoughts

Perhaps no other figure in the history of the Ukrainian Orthodox Church is as controversial as Metropolitan Petro Mohyla. For traditionalists within the Orthodox Church, Mohyla is primarily an opportunist. The most vocal advocate of this opinion was the respected Father Florovsky, who wrote:

---

89 Florovskii, p. 50.
90 Popivchak, p. 51.

> Petr Mogila's attitude to the problems of the Roman Catholic Church was clear and simple. He did not see any real differences between Orthodoxy and Rome. He was convinced of the importance of canonical independence, but perceived no threat from inner "Latinization." Indeed he welcomed it and promoted it. . . . Under such conditions, Orthodoxy lost its inner independence, as well as its measuring rod of self-examination. . . . Mogila contributed more than any other . . . to the entrenchment of "crypto-Romanism" in the life of the West Russian Church.[91]

Current views expressed by the Eastern Catholics, especially Ukrainian Catholics, are very similar, in that most are positive in reviewing Mohyla's quasi-Orthodox theology. Mohyla would, of course, appeal to a Church which has adopted many Roman Catholic beliefs, yet practices an Eastern ritual. Father Ronald Popivchak, a Ukrainian Catholic priest, supported this view when he wrote: "The *Confession* of Peter Mohila is an authentic reflection of the theology of the Eastern Church."[92] From this statement,

---

91 Florovskii, p. 51.
92 Popivchak, p. 226.

found at the conclusion of Popivchak's analysis of Mohyla's *Confession*, one would be led to believe that the theology of the Eastern (i.e., Orthodox) Church is extremely similar, in many cases, to Roman Catholic theology. That, for this writer, is not the case.

The highly respected Timothy Ware, now Bishop Kallistos of Diokleia, probably represents the majority of modern Orthodox thought about Petro Mohyla when he states that, although accepted during a difficult period in the history of the Orthodox Church and written as an answer to Lukaris' Calvinistic *Confession*, "the Orthodox Confession of Moghila represents the high-water mark of Latin influence upon Orthodox theology."[93]

The view of Ukrainian historians concerning Mohyla, his rule over the Kyivan Church, and his *Confession* are all quite similarly positive. Mohyla represents a period when the Kyivan Church was strong and influential in world Orthodoxy. This was a time when the Church was most important for those seeking less Russian dominance and influence over Ukraine, Mohyla represented an anti-Russian stance, although perhaps a pro-Polish one. The first president of an independent Ukraine in the twentieth century and historian, Mykhailo

---

93 Ware, *Eustratios Argenti*, p. 13.

Hrushev'ky wrote that "Mohyla truly prepared the ground for an independent Ukrainian patriarchate."[94]

The fairest analysis and explanation of Mohyla's actions and theology is given by the highly respected theologian and Church historian, Jaroslav Pelikan, who himself was a Lutheran[95] when he wrote about Mohyla. Pelikan analyzes Mohyla as one who combined two theological methods in his statement of Eastern doctrines: The repetition of ancient truths in ancient words and the response to contemporary challenges in words appropriate to them. Such an approach is usually difficult and has often been condemned in Eastern Orthodox thought. "To grasp the Eastern understanding of the church and of its doctrine, one has to return from the schoolroom to the worshipping Church and perhaps to change the school dialect of theology for the pictorial and metaphorical language of Scripture."[96]

In a convincing essay written by Professor Ihor Sevcenko, entitled "The Many Worlds of Petro Mohyla," there is an appeal to keep the verdict of Mohyla's contemporaries in mind"[97] when analyzing the theology of the Metropolitan of Kyiv. What is, however, questionable, is the statement of Sevcenko

---

94 M. Hrushev'ky, *Z Istorii Relihinoii Dumky na Ukraini* (Winnipeg: Ukrains'ke Evanhel's'ke Obyednannia, 1962), p. 91.

95 Pelikan later became a member of the Orthodox Church.

96 Pelikan, p. 295.

97 Sevcenko, pp. 33-34.

concerning Mohyla's *Confession*: "in this approved form, the document was highly valued and accepted as the official profession of faith by all the leaders of Orthodox churches of the seventeenth and eighteenth centuries."[98]

It is true that Mohyla's *Confession* remains on the list of chief Orthodox doctrinal statements written since 787, but only in its revised form, a form which Mohyla did not fully accept. The question then is whether or not the *Confession* was highly valued and accepted by Mohyla's contemporaries. Professor Sevcenko, in his article, offers no proof or defense of such a statement other than the fact that it remained on the list of approved catechisms of the Orthodox Church. Certainly, the *Confession* of Dositheos of 1672, although also containing certain Latinisms, remains closer to Orthodox theology and Eastern thought.

It was important for Orthodoxy to express its mind concerning the topics being raised by the Reformation controversies and to define its position in relation to the new teachings which had arisen in the West. Although such statements by Mohyla did answer questions about Orthodox theology raised by Roman Catholics, Eastern Catholics, and Protestants, they were answered for the most part falsely, especially considering the Patristic and contemporary Orthodox teaching on these various issues. For the Orthodox there are numerous

---

[98] Ibid., p. 35.

times that in order to maintain an Orthodox consciousness, it remains better not to answer questions about the unknown, the divine, with mere human thought and human language.

The question remains: Why did Mohyla continue to be loyal to his original "western" theology, after his *Confession* had been revised by the highest temporal body of the Orthodox Church, second only to an Ecumenical council or local council? Perhaps Mohyla was not familiar with traditional, patristic thought and theology, which an Orthodox Christian believes has the ability to answer theological questions. Such thought, produced during the first eight centuries of Christianity, also provides within its body the possibility of declining to answer unanswerable questions.

Mohyla, although Metropolitan of Kyiv, was, as are all Orthodox bishops, subject to the authority and decisions of councils, such as the one in Iasi which changed and ratified his *Confession*. Thus, one must come either to the conclusion that Mohyla disagreed with patristic and contemporary Orthodox thought and practice and kept to his own version of Orthodox theology, or was ignorant of most patristic thought and chose to pursue his own methods of explaining Orthodox doctrine. It is hard to imagine that Mohyla was not familiar or could not have been advised on Orthodox patristic theology; perhaps Florovsky is correct in viewing Mohyla as a power-hungry crypto-Romanist. The question remains if such power blinded his view of pure Orthodox thought.

To be sure, the *Orthodox Confession of Faith* by Petro Mohyla needs to be viewed in its seventeenth century context. To use the document today as a defense of Orthodox theology, or as a response to Protestant or Roman Catholic criticism, would be a betrayal of Orthodox thought. Rather, the document has its real importance and relevance as a historical treatise of the living faith. Today, Petro Mohyla needs to be seen as a leader of a confused and shattered Church, who kept the spirit alive by contributing, although with great human frailty, to Her sanctity.

Frequently Works Cited

Cavarnos, Constantine. *The Future Life According to Orthodox Teaching*. Etna, California: Center for Traditionalist Orthodox Studies, 1985.

Chadwick, Henry. *The Early Church*. London: Penguin Books, 1967.

Charipova, Liudmila. "Peter Mohyla's Translation of The Imitation of Christ" *The Historical Journal*. Vol. 46, No. 2 (2003): 237-261.

Davies, Norman. *God's Playground: A History of Poland*. New York: Columbia University Press, 1982.

Florovskii, Georgii. *Puti Russkago Bogosloviia*. Paris: YMCA Press, 1983.

Golubev, Stefan. *Kievskii Mitropolit Petr Mogila i Ego Spodvizhniki*. Kyiv: Korchak-Novitski, 1883.

Hrushevs'ky, Mykhailo. *Z Istorii Relihinoi Dumky na Ukraini*. Winnipeg: Ukrains'ke Evanhel's'ke Obyednannia, 1962.

John (St.) of Damascus. "Exposition of the Orthodox Faith" in *The Nicene and Post-Nicene Fathers*, edited by W. Sanday. Vol. IX. Grand Rapids, Michigan: Eerdmans Publishing Co., 1979.

Joukovsky, Arcady. *Petro Mohyla I Pytannia Iednosty Tserkov.* Paris: Ukrains'ky Vil'ny Universytet, 1969.

Kharlampovich, K. *Malorossiskoe Vliianie na Velykorysskyiu Tserkovnyiu Zhyzn.* Kazan: 1914.

Kyprian, (archimandrit). *Evkharystiia.* Paris: YMCA Press, 1947.

Le Goff, Jacques. The Birth of Purgatory. Chicago: The University of Chicago, 1981.

Lewin, Paulina. "The Kiev Mohyla Academy in Relation to Polish Culture." *Harvard Ukrainian Studies.* Vol. VIII, No. 1/2 (June 1984): 123-135.

Maloney, George A. *A History of Orthodox Theology since 1453.* Belmont, Massachusetts: Noland Publishing Co., 1976.

Pelikan, Jaroslav. *The Growth of Medieval Theology 600-1300.* Chicago: The University of Chicago, 1978.

Popivchak, Ronald P. Peter Mohila, Metropolitan of Kiev (1663-1647) *Translation and Evaluation of His "Orthodox Confession of Faith"* (1640). Washington D.C.: The Catholic University of America, 1975.

Potichnyj, Peter J., ed. *Poland and Ukraine, Past and Present.* Edmonton: The Canadian Institute of Ukrainian Studies, 1980.

Staniforth, Maxwell, trans. *Early Christian Writings.* Middlesex: Penguin Books, 1968.

Robertson, J. trans. *The Acts and Decrees of the Synod of Jerusalem*. London: 1899.

Sevcenko, Ihor. "The Many Worlds of Peter Mohyla." *Harvard Ukrainian Studies*. Vol. VIII, No. 1/2 (June 1984): 9-44.

Sydorenko, Alexander. *The Kievan Academy in the Seventeenth Century*. Ottawa: The University of Ottawa Press, 1977.

Sysyn, Frank E. "Peter Mohyla and the Kiev Academy in Recent Western Works: Divergent Views on Seventeenth Century Ukrainian Culture." *Harvard Ukrainian Studies*. Vol. VIII, No. 1/2 (June 1984): 155-187.

Vlasovs'ky, Ivan. *Narys Istorii Ukrains'koi Pravoslavnoi Tserkvy*. Vol. 2 of 4 in 5, New York: Ukrainian Orthodox Church, 1956.

Ware, Timothy. *Eustratios Argenti. A Study of the Greek Church Under Turkish Rule*. Oxford: Clarendon Press, 1964.

Ware, Timothy. *The Orthodox Church*. Middlesex: Penguin Books, 1963.

Wenger, A. "La reconciliation des heretiques dans l'Eglise Russe." *Revue des Etudes Byzantines*. Vol. XII (195): 144-175.

Image Credits

Cover http://www.encyclopediaofukraine.com
Page 3 http://www.encyclopediaofukraine.com
Page 5 *Kievskaia Starina* 1882
Page 7 http://colectieicoane.blogspot.com/2011_09_01_archive.html
Page 9 http://www.stamp.kiev.ua/ukr/stamp/?p=1&fi=1&rubrID=12
Page 11 http://www.posta.md/en/filatelia.html
Page 14 http://de.wikipedia.org/wiki/Petro_Mohyla
Page 15 http://www.encyclopediaofukraine.com
Page 19 http://www.encyclopediaofukraine.com
Page 20 http://www.encyclopediaofukraine.com
Page 27 http://www.encyclopediaofukraine.com
Page 28 http://www.encyclopediaofukraine.com
Page 30 **http://www.coinarchives.com**
Page 34 http://commons.wikimedia.org
Page 37 **http://www.encyclopediaofukraine.com**

www.ingramcontent.com/pod-product-compliance
Lightning Source LLC
Chambersburg PA
CBHW031418040426
42444CB00005B/626